SandCastle

Word Families Set 5

-ob as in knob

Amanda Rondeau

Consulting Editor Monica Marx, M.A./Reading Specialist

ABDO Publishing Company

Published by SandCastle™, an imprint of ABDO Publishing Company, 4940 Viking Drive, Edina, Minnesota 55435.

Printed in the United States.

Credits
Edited by: Pam Price
Curriculum Coordinator: Nancy Tuminelly
Cover and Interior Design and Production: Mighty Media
Photo Credits: Comstock, Eyewire Images, Hemera, PhotoDisc

Library of Congress Cataloging-in-Publication Data

Rondeau, Amanda, 1974-
    -Ob as in knob / Amanda Rondeau.
       p. cm. -- (Word families. Set V)
    Summary: Introduces, in brief text and illustrations, the use of the letter combination "ob" in such words as "knob," "mob," "fob," and "blob."
    ISBN 1-59197-249-3
    1. Readers (Primary) [1. Vocabulary. 2. Reading.] I. Title.

PE1119 .R693 2003
428.1--dc21
                                                                                    2002038228

SandCastle™ books are created by a professional team of educators, reading specialists, and content developers around five essential components that include phonemic awareness, phonics, vocabulary, text comprehension, and fluency. All books are written, reviewed, and leveled for guided reading, early intervention reading, and Accelerated Reader® programs and designed for use in shared, guided, and independent reading and writing activities to support a balanced approach to literacy instruction.

Let Us Know

After reading the book, SandCastle would like you to tell us your stories about reading. What is your favorite page? Was there something hard that you needed help with? Share the ups and downs of learning to read. We want to hear from you! To get posted on the ABDO Publishing Company Web site, send us e-mail at:

sandcastle@abdopub.com

SandCastle Level: Transitional

-ob Words

bob

cob

job

knob

mob

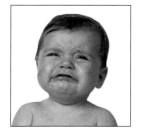

sob

The floats bob in the water.

Maggie is cleaning
corn on the cob.

Chris has a job as a chef.

Dan's shoulder is as high as the knob.

There was a mob of people at the parade.

Ben sat at his desk to
sob.

Bob Was a Slob

Bob was an awful slob!

Cleaning was his
least favorite job.

Bob's dad said, "Bob,
why are you such a slob?"

"No one will want
to visit a room like
this, Bob!"

13

Bob thought his dad
was being a snob.

But then friends stopped
visiting Bob.

Bob got so lonely
he started to sob.

"Cleaning is now
too big of a job!"

17

But all of his friends
came in a mob.

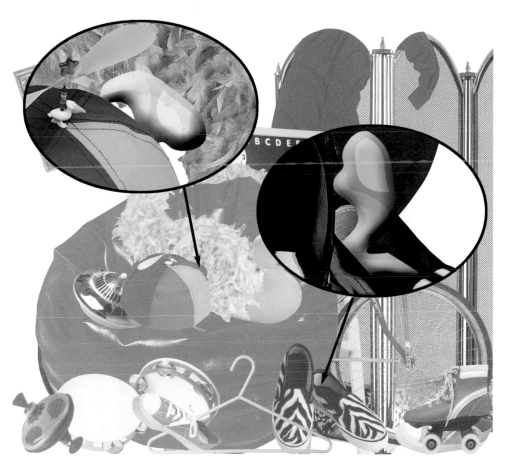

They picked up the blob.

They wiped up a glob.

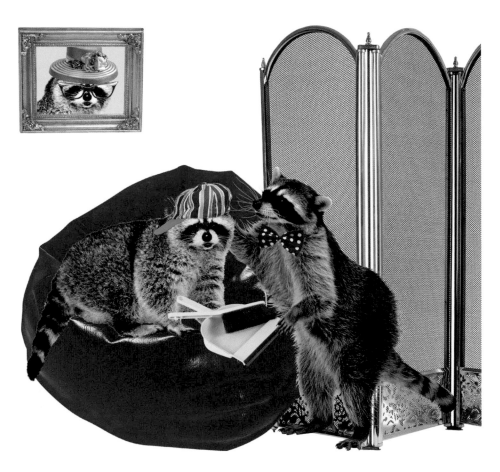

Bob is no longer a slob.

Cleaning is now
his favorite job!

The -ob Word Family

blob	lob
bob	mob
cob	rob
fob	slob
glob	snob
job	sob
knob	

Glossary

Some of the words in this list may have more than one meaning. The meaning listed here reflects the way the word is used in the book.

chef   a cook at a restaurant

clean   to put things away and remove dirt

lonely   feeling sad and alone

parade   a public procession done as a celebration

shoulder   the joint that connects the upper arm and body

snob   a person who thinks he or she is better than other people

About SandCastle™

A professional team of educators, reading specialists, and content developers created the SandCastle™ series to support young readers as they develop reading skills and strategies and increase their general knowledge. The SandCastle™ series has four levels that correspond to early literacy development in young children. The levels are provided to help teachers and parents select the appropriate books for young readers.

Emerging Readers
(no flags)

Beginning Readers
(1 flag)

Transitional Readers
(2 flags)

Fluent Readers
(3 flags)

These levels are meant only as a guide. All levels are subject to change.

To see a complete list of SandCastle™ books and other nonfiction titles from ABDO Publishing Company, visit **www.abdopub.com** or contact us at:

4940 Viking Drive, Edina, Minnesota 55435 • 1-800-800-1312 • fax: 1-952-831-1632